The Quee[n]
the Cast[le]

Written by Lisa Thompson

Pictures by Andy Hamilton

The Queen had a big ring.

She had a big throne.

She had a big crown.

CROWN
POLISH

She had a big bed.

She had a big dress.

She had a big horse.

The King had to make a big, BIG castle.

Think About!
Why did the King have to make a big, BIG castle?
What big things does the Queen have?
What big thing would you like to own?